Steam Memories on Shed: 1950's – 1960's

No. 26: Western Region Engine S

Photographs by the late **K R PIRT D DALTON & D BEECROFT**

Copyright Book Law Publications 2011
ISBN 978-1-907094-61-3

INTRODUCTION

This album contains the work of three photographers who all had a passion for railways and recorded some memorable images which we today can enjoy and hopefully travel back in time to a period when steam locomotion still ruled on British Railways. The photographers are Don Beecroft, David Dalton and Keith Pirt and the subject covers Western Region engine sheds and their motive power. The compiler has tried to cover, geographically, the whole of what became the Western Region of British Railways but such was its size it is impossible to represent every corner and nook and cranny in an album of this stature. That said, we have plenty of variety from the typical branchline to the huge roundhouses. The Cambrian lines have been represented by images captured by Keith Pirt during his lifelong affection for the area. Our other photographers have managed to leave us with some stunning views of which most, if not all, are previously unpublished. After looking through the album and digesting the captions the reader might ask themselves one thing 'Where has it all gone?' They are images from the past, so enjoy them but be warned, they are full of memories and nostalgia!

Cover Picture

An interior view of Tyseley in July 1958 with visiting 2-8-2T No.7232 rubbing shoulders with the local 2-6-2Ts. *Keith Pirt.*

Title Page Picture

'Dukedog' No.9004 rests at the north headshunt of Croes Newydd engine shed on 12th July 1959. Two of this class were allocated to 84J at this time - No.9014 being the other. A third engine, No.9018 had just transferred to Oswestry. Both of the 4-4-0s ended their days at Croes Newydd in June and October 1960 respectively. The latter engine, along with the withdrawal of Machynlleth's No.9017, at the same time, saw the class become extinct on British Railways although No.9017 did eventually pass into preservation. Most of their work was over the former Cambrian lines although the lightly laid Didcot, Newbury and Southampton route did require the services of a handful of the class until that line was upgraded to allow the passage of heavier locomotive types. *David Dalton.*

Printed and bound by The Amadeus Press, Cleckheaton, West Yorkshire
First published in the United Kingdom by Book Law Publications, 382 Carlton Hill, Nottingham, NG4 1JA

This is the engine shed at Fairford terminus, situated at the end of the 22 mile long branch from Yarnton Junction on the Oxford to Worcester main line. The branch was opened in two stages by two separate companies. The first part, from Yarnton Junction to Witney was completed November 1861, by the Witney Railway Co. and an engine shed was erected at the original terminus in Witney. In 1869 the East Gloucestershire Railway started work on the Witney to Fairford stretch and that section opened in January 1873. Although two long sidings, both approximately a quarter mile long, can be seen in this 17th March 1962 photograph, the original layout had just one (on which the brakevan stands) and that was to become the running line of the planned continuation to Cirencester and Cheltenham. The second siding was laid during W.W.II when a number of airfields and military camps were established in the area. Indeed, such was the activity during the period of the conflict that in October 1944 a station was built at Carterton between Brize Norton and Alvescot to serve the nearby airfield; other stations had passing loops laid along with extra sidings whilst Eynsham acquired a second platform. When fully operational in 1873, the whole branch was operated by the Great Western Railway who supplied four return passenger services a day between Oxford and Fairford; the GWR eventually absorbed the two local concerns in July 1890. The engine shed, as can be seen, was of timber construction and opened in January 1873 when, at the same time, the Witney engine shed was closed. 0-6-0PT No.3653 has just replenished its tank and was about to turn on the 55ft turntable, another legacy of the war when the original 45ft device was enlarged to allow larger tender engines to work right along the branch with military loads. Just to the right of the engine can be seen a grounded horsebox wagon body which served as a mess room for the engine crews up to closure. The shed itself remained open to the end in June 1962, not quite attaining its ninetieth birthday. *David Dalton.*

3

No.3653 calls for water at the conical tank where another 'Pannier' No.7445 has just finished with the bag. The turntable pit can just be seen between No.3653 and the line of mineral wagons. Oxford shed supplied the motive power for the branch from opening and 2-2-2 tender engines worked the passenger services up to WW1, hence the requirement for a 45ft TT. Other types employed included the 2-4-0 'Metro' tanks which worked the line for many years until 1949 when the last of them, No.3588, was withdrawn. Latterly 22XX class 0-6-0 tender engines brought to and took goods trains away from the branch but the 0-6-0PT was the real workhorse of the line running all the passenger services. Over the years many of them have plied the route to and from Oxford but contemporary observations have shown that Nos.3653, 7404, 7411, 7412, 7445, 9653, 9654 were regulars during the final few years of the line's operation. However, 14XX 0-4-2Ts did on occasion work some passenger trains but their limited water capacity apparently made them far from ideal motive power on the branch. After reaching a peak during W.W.II, passenger services reverted to four return passenger trains each weekday between Oxford and Fairford along with a single daily goods to Fairford and one to Witney, both from Oxford. Four sets of men stationed at Fairford shed handled approximately half the trains on the branch in latter years. *David Dalton.*

This view of Fairford station on that 17th day of March 1962 is included simply to show the size of the terminus which the EGR did not envisage as being of a permanent nature. Alas their plans to continue the line to Cirencester never came to anything, the buffer stops beside the engine shed marking the physical end of the railway. In this picture we see 'Pannier' No.3653 about to pull away from the single platform station which in reality was not much bigger than a halt albeit with all the necessary infrastructure of a terminus but on a very small scale by comparison. The 0-6-0PT would proceed past the camera, pulling its two coaches clear of the points, uncouple, move on to the engine shed where any necessary servicing was carried out. After using the turntable it would run past its train as far as the station where it would set back, couple up and draw its train into the platform for the return to Oxford. So we leave Fairford behind shortly before its inevitable closure; another branchline falling victim to decline. The last day of the passenger service was on Saturday 16th June 1962 with official closure of the Witney to Fairford (EGR) section taking place on the following Monday, 18th June. The Oxford to Witney line, using the original terminus at the latter place, was served by goods trains until 2nd November 1970 when it too was closed. *David Dalton.* 5

The engine shed at St Philips Marsh in Bristol consisted two roundhouses built in typical Great Western style and opened in 1910. The complement of engines during BR days consisted numerous tank engines (sixty or more 'Pannier' tanks for instance), dozens of mixed traffic tender engines (Halls and Granges), along with eight-coupled heavy freight locomotives or both GW and WD origin. There was even a couple of 47XX 2-8-0s resident for much of the Fifties. Besides the ubiquitous 0-6-0PT, which were supplied to all the yards in the area, some of the main line freight traffic was handled by some of these large 2-8-0Ts, one of which, No.4262, was part of the complement up to the end of 1957. No.4248 was however a visitor from Ebbw Junction and had worked into Bristol with a freight via the Severn tunnel on this gloomy 16th day of August 1958. *David Dalton.*

Just across the yard from No.4248 on that same day was another of 86A's eight-coupled tanks - 2-8-2T No.7245 - stabled with yet another 2-8-0T. Once again St Philips Marsh had representatives of this class allocated in the shape of No.7250, from September 1952 to September 1957, No.7201 from September 1951 to December 1954, and No.7241 from April 1954 to April 1955. As a generalisation it would be safe to say that most of the 2-8-2 tank engines were allocated to engine sheds in south Wales where they were employed on the heavy mineral trains originating in the coal mining districts of the Welsh Valleys but Others could be found in Oxfordshire where they worked iron-ore trains and other heavy freight. In June 1954 St Philips Marsh once again became home for a batch of Stanier 2-8-0s (all Swindon built examples of course) when a dozen or so 8Fs were drafted in, including eight from the London Midland Region. Of course the class were no strangers to the former GWR lines in Bristol as a fair number had been allocated to SPM when new during W.W.II. In this view of the south side of the shed yard we can see the neglect and dilapidation that was already prevalent on BR at this period. No doubt Churchward or Collett would have had something to say about the weed growth and the rubbish strewn about in an operational motive power depot such as this. SPM closed to steam in June 1964 and the twin roundhouses were later demolished to make way for a depot servicing diesel units. *David Dalton.* 7

An undated view of one of the largely nocturnal 47XX 2-8-0s outside the south roundhouse at SPM. The engine is No.4704, one of the Old Oak Common batch and appears to be in something of a diabolical external condition so this may well be towards its withdrawal in May 1964. The 56XX class No.6678, just visible on the left, was still active to November 1964 albeit not at St Philips Marsh. One of the 47XX 2-8-0s, No.4700, had already been withdrawn at SPM in October 1962 but was still stored awaiting removal in June 1963. The withdrawal of No.4704, along with 4703 and 4707, would render this class extinct - none were preserved! *David Dalton.*

Bristol's other GW engine shed, 82A, was sited nearer to the main passenger station which enabled the motive power to slip in and out with greater ease and relieved line occupation around Temple Meads. Known as Bath Road, the depot was situated between the ancient thoroughfare and the River Avon. The shed's six-coupled motive power consisted examples of all that was best on the former GWR/ WR - Kings, Castles, Saints, Halls and Counties. In our picture here, captured on 16th August 1958, none of the above named classes are represented and instead we have to make do with a BR Standard Cl.3 tank, and a 43XX 2-6-0 tender engine possibly No.6363; both are, alas, unidentified but examples of their kind were allocated to 82A at this time as were the small and large examples of 'Prairie' tank. It is one of the latter which is stealing centre stage in this view but, ironically, it is not one of Bath Road's own. Instead we have to make do with No.4135, an ex-works example making its way back home to Pontypool Road from Swindon. Bath Road engine shed had been in existence since the Bristol & Exeter Railway had erected their shed here in 1850 but the building in view stems from 1934 when the Great Western had demolished and replaced an earlier (1877) GWR roundhouse with this glass gabled ten-road structure paid for by a Government loan. In September 1960 this shed too was demolished to make way for a diesel depot, the steam motive power being banished to St Philips Marsh and the former Midland establishment at Barrow Road. *David Dalton.*

9

Cheltenham Malvern Road engine shed was opened in 1907 to replace a shed sited nearer to Cheltenham (St James) passenger station. Originally of just two roads - the brick building immediately behind the two locomotives - the shed was extended on its north side in 1943 by the addition of a two road structure constructed of corrugated asbestos on a lightweight steel frame; part of the gable is just visible on the left of this 16th August 1958 picture. On shed this Saturday are Gloucester Horton Road's 45XX No.4573, and Swindon's 43XX No.5351. Interestingly a passenger station which was appropriately named Cheltenham Spa (Malvern Road) was erected opposite the new engine shed in on 30th March 1908. However, as a wartime cost saving measure the station was closed during the whole of 1917 and 1918 but re-opened for business on 1st July 1919. It finally closed on 3rd January 1966 along with the terminal station at St James. The engine shed itself closed during October 1963 and after a period of disuse was let out to a private concern. *David Dalton.*

(*opposite*) A more southerly aspect of the shed in September 1956 with more of the 'new' two-road corrugated asbestos section on view, albeit behind a small 2-6-2T No.5518. *D.H.Beecroft.*

Its proximity to the locomotives workshops brought many visiting engines onto Swindon running shed. Many after overhaul but most came during the daily round of traffic requirements. This is former ROD 2-8-0 No.3028 of Oxley shed is stabled on Swindon shed yard on 6th May 1956, just weeks before it was condemned and broken up, apparently at Swindon works. In this view the 2-8-0 appears healthy enough and the tender is full as though departure back to Wolverhampton is imminent, even the wheels treads are nice and shiny. At the start of the year Oxley had a handful of these 7F engines but they got rid of more than half of the complement during the summer to withdrawal and managed to get rid of the rest by November when the last ones were transferred away to South Wales depots. Unchanged since their somewhat cheap acquisition from the Ministry of Supply, this Robinson design was one which the GWR got great value for money, over and over again. Although August 1956 was the end for this engine, the last three members of the Western Region contingent lasted until withdrawal in October 1958. Behind the engine is the last of Swindon's roundhouse sheds and indeed the last of its locomotives sheds which was built in 1908. Closure for the depot took place in October 1964. *David Dalton.*

An undated BR period photograph of a long line of engines at Risca, north-west of Newport, where neither engine shed or stabling point were ever established. Therefore the only conclusion is a line of withdrawn engines awaiting entry to Bird's scrapyard. Although mainly of GWR origin, there is one Stanier tender at the top of the line which helps to reinforce the theory of a line of condemned locomotives awaiting their fate. *David Dalton.*

A nice busy aspect of Plymouth Laira shed yard on 27th July 1958 with some heavyweight motive power gracing the depot. The covered accommodation here comprised a four-road straight shed - opened in 1931 - which was attached to a 1901 brick-built roundhouse which had a somewhat low profile roof compared with the majority of GWR square roundhouse sheds being put up during this period. However, space was always a problem at Laira in steam days so that by weekend, after the summer Saturday workings were completed, the yard was certainly bulging with buffer to buffer engines. This was another depot which had representatives from all the major passenger classes, in most cases substantial. A handful of the larger freight engines were also allocated to 83D, including the WD 'Austerity' 2-8-0. Listing the named classes shows what was on offer to visitors during the Fifties': Kings, Castles, Stars, Counties, Hall, Granges, Manors. Even after the diesels had arrived in 1959/60 and taken over the straight shed, the list of resident named classes still ran to a respectable six with only the solitary 'Star' missing; it was in fact condemned at Swindon in December 1951. The former Taunton based 43XX No.5321 was of course a visitor and was en route to Llanelly on transfer - the long way round. *David Dalton.*

The east end of Slough engine shed during its rebuilding in 1954. This four road shed started life as a goods shed and was created because of the remodelling of the adjacent junction in 1868, when the original one-road shed of 1840s vintage was demolished. As can be seen in this view, besides the roof work, the end gables are being bricked-in, although the contractors are making something of a meal about the job judging by the amount of soot staining the new brickwork where scaffolding is still erected. The work was eventually finished and both ends then had brick in-fill on cast in situ concrete beams. Only three roads projected from this the north-eastern end because the original goods office was kept and used by the Running Dept. It is possible to make out which part of the building was the pre-1868 goods shed, the large openings in the dividing wall also giving something of a clue. To the right of the gabled shed, and hiding behind the 43XX, can be seen a lean-to shed which was erected in 1935 to house the diesel railcars that were being introduced by the GWR. Situated on the south side of the Windsor branch, the engine shed housed a large number of tank locomotives, of varying sizes, used on the local suburban services and those along the main line to Paddington. At this time in the mid-50s the allocation consisted about forty engines of which half were 'Panniers' of different vintages, including the latest version from the 94XX series, a couple of 14XX 0-4-2T for branch work, and approximately twenty of the large 'Prairie' tanks of the 61XX class. The exact date was 31st January and the visiting tender engine was a Reading based 2-6-0, No.9315. Coded 81B by British Railways, Slough eventually went the way of all steam motive power depots and was closed on the first day of June 1964. *KRP 150.*

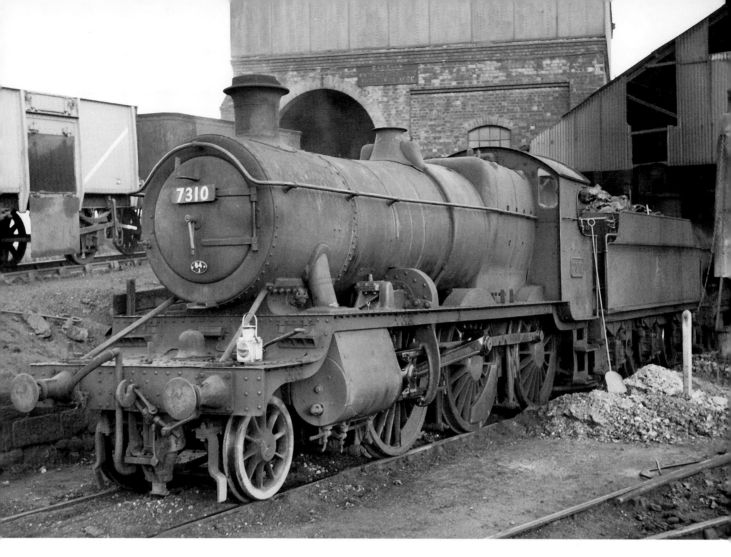

Looking very tired, 43XX class No.7310 appears to be in need of a trip to Swindon or Wolverhampton for an overhaul. It is 31st October 1954 and Croes Newydd shed had about a dozen of these mixed traffic 2-6-0s on its books. The depot here comprised a square roundhouse situated in the triangle created by the west, north and south junctions at Croes Newydd, Wrexham. Built in 1902, the roundhouse unusually had a northlight roof rather than the lofty roof spaces normally associated with GWR roundhouses. A new roof was required in 1924 so it is assumed that a catastrophic event such as a fire must have occurred because new roofs were not usually need after just twenty-two years of service, even on an engine shed. We are looking here up the wagon ramp at the western face of the coaling stage, whilst at ground level a rather dilapidated steel framed corrugated asbestos shed, erected at some time during W.W.II, gives some semblance of cover for engine servicing. Scenes such as these remind us of the ever present dirt and filth which was found at every steam locomotive shed, large or small. This depot was still operational when the London Midland Region took control in September 1963 and changed its code to 6C, the first BR code 84J having changed in January 1961 to 89B. The transfer to the LMR gave the place a temporary 'new lease of life' and the closure of Croes Newydd (New Cross in English) did not take place until June 1967 when the remaining allocation - mainly BR Standards - were sent to other depots. *KRP 27H.8.5.*

Craven Arms was another former L&NWR engine shed which became part of the Western Region shortly after nationalisation. Although situated on the Joint line between Shrewsbury and Hereford, the shed did not become GWR property because the L&NWR built their own route - the Central Wales line - from a junction at Craven Arms to Swansea. This depot therefore was to serve the needs of the LNW rather than Joint line requirements. The four road shed was opened for business in 1869 in a hipped roof style then popular with the Premier Line architects. Note, even in BR days, the delicate looking ventilators rising from the original slated roof with its central ventilator still intact. The Fowler 2-6-4T was typical of the motive power used for passenger services on the Central Wales line, the numerous stations - even now - requiring lots of stop start situations which suited this class of engine. Even in LNWR days the 4-6-2 tank engines built for suburban passenger traffic flourished on this line. The goods traffic was handled by the former LNWR 7F 0-8-0 tender engines which only gave up the job in BR days to the Stanier 8F. This undated photograph gives us no clues as to why the 'Dukedog' is stabled but some wag has placed a child's' toy horse on the lamp iron, much like a headboard. The Fowler tank carries a Swansea Paxton St. 87K shed plate but it transferred from there to Landore in October 1959, when Paxton St. closed. No.9014 carries no shed plate but transferred from 89C to 84J in June 1957. Therefore it could have been seconded by Shrewsbury shed whilst en route from the coast to Wrexham? Closed in May 1964, this engine shed was still standing, albeit derelict, ten years later, therefore attaining its one hundredth birthday without any major alteration, especially to its roof. *David Dalton.*

This picture featuring 'Castle' No.5042, with what appears to be its driver in conversation with shed management, at the outlet from Old Oak Common shed on 14th May 1961, could well be a contender for a caption competition - perhaps! My favourite would have been - Driver, with fag in mouth, on the left. "So, what d'you fink? The tenders' full of them ovaltine fing's so a decent lump or two of coal might elp." Running Foreman, with hands on hips. "If you can get them up there, they're yours!" There are others which spring to mind but I'll leave you to your own thoughts. Meanwhile, WINCHESTER CASTLE waits patiently for the road to Paddington to work a Down afternoon express which could be virtually anywhere on the Region from Plymouth to Chester and everywhere in between those points. The Fireman seems to be tending to his duties on the footplate whilst the Driver has a natter with the Foreman! Whoops! That's' where we came in. *David Dalton.*

Old Oak Common 25th May 1955 - 'Castle' No.7009 ATHELNEY CASTLE attends the coaling stage after working into Paddington with the early morning express from Swansea. Behind is 'Britannia' No.70023 VENUS, which had come on shed just before the 4-6-0 after being released from a morning express it had brought in from Cardiff. The procession of locomotives coming on shed at OOC and requiring coal seemed endless to the layman but for the coalmen it must have been more like purgatory - a never ending conveyor belt! This particular coaling stage was the largest which the GWR built and is what the stages at Ebbw Junction and Oxley would have become had they been enlarged. Built in 1906, this building sufficed at Old Oak Common until steam was eliminated from the depot in March 1965. *Ron Hodge.*

Wolverhampton's Stafford Road engine shed was something of a rambling place which always looked somewhat more neglected than the average engine shed. However, when the sun came out, as in this 11th May 1958 view in the yard, things didn't appear too bad. Add a nicely cleaned locomotive and you have a pleasing picture to bring back happy memories in years to come. It was of course a Sunday so there were not many people about and assuming you were not part of an organised 'shed bash' you could take your time and savour the place for what it was - as a home and repair shop for steam locomotives. Resident 'Castle' No.5026 CRICCIETH CASTLE is awaiting Monday morning attention to its inside valve gear on which, more than likely, a start has just been made on the repair or, perhaps a finish is in sight. The tender is full of choice coal so the 4-6-0 must have failed just prior to taking up an express duty to Paddington. *David Dalton.*

84A - February 1963. This picture was taken in virtually the same place as the previous Stafford Road view, certainly on the same stretch of track. But, nearly five years on, the mood has changed dramatically now and it is one of desperation. Two unidentified members of the depot's once proud 'King' class wait in the icy surrounds of the shed yard for the final tow to the scrapyard. The engines have been stripped of anything of value to souvenir hunters - they are called 'collectors' now - and all that remains is perhaps the copper cap of the chimney. Stafford Road shed closed seven months after this scene was captured. The remaining engines went to Oxley shed and the whole site was demolished and cleared. The place was one of BR's eyesores, even by the industrial standards of the West Midlands. *David Dalton.* 21

Another view of Stafford Road in 1963 with further dilapidation evident. We are looking into one of the roundhouses, past a withdrawn and barely twelve years old 0-6-0T - No.8428. This former Oxley engine was condemned in October 1962 and has conveniently been dumped in the southern section of Stafford Road shed yard where little movement of anything took place and was the ideal dumping ground; the youngster did at least have some exalted company during its long wait for the call to the scrap yard. *David Dalton.*

Bodmin's single road engine shed in September 1960 with St Blazey's 45XX 2-6-2T No.4565 resting outside. Besides this engine, St Blazey also supplied Nos.4559, 4569, 4584, and 4585 amongst others at various times to run the passenger service between Bodmin (Road), General and Wadebridge. The shed was opened by the GWR in 1887 and was situated at the south end of Bodmin (General) station on the west side of the line. As can be gleaned from the illustration, a coaling stage of sorts, and a conical top circular water tank completed the facilities. Closed in April 1962, the shed had great promise for preservation when it was leased to a railway preservation group but BR took the building back, demolished it and then apparently, eventually sold the site to another railway preservation group who have plans to rebuild a similar type of engine shed. *Don Beecroft.*

23

Kingham engine shed dated from 1913 when the GWR decided to replace an earlier timber-built shed which had been closed in 1906. Originally called Chipping Norton Junction, the engine shed had stood approximately where the concrete lamp standard is located on the island platform here. Brick-built, and comprising a single road like its predecessor, the new shed had a turntable and small coaling stage befitting its small allocation. Standing in the fork of the main line to Worcester and the branch from Kingham to Chipping Norton, the shed was closed in December 1962. The station here was opened in 1855 and was also called Chipping Norton Junction until renamed in 1909. Today the station survives on the double line section of the route from Oxford to Worcester, a line singled many years ago but which is now undergoing a doubling in a change of fortune which hopefully will continue. In this view one of Kingham's regular residents, 'Prairie' No.5173, wheels its Oxford-bound stopping train off the curve of the line from Chipping Norton on 17th March 1962. That one-time branchline - also opened in August 1855 - was extended north-eastwards in 1887 from Chipping Norton to Kings Sutton on the Oxford-Birmingham main line but like many rural lines in post-war Britain, it became a victim of the Beeching axe and closed on 3rd December 1962 whereby the reason for the engine shed's existence disappeared, its closure inevitable. Also in view, on the embankment immediately behind the engine shed, is the connecting line from Cheltenham to the Birmingham line which by-passed Kingham's junction and was constructed at about the time of the extension to Kings Sutton. The junction of the line to Cheltenham, out of picture to the left, enjoyed the same fate as the route to Kings Sutton but it closed a little earlier - 15th October 1962. As a modelling project this particular location offers a bit more than the once popular GWR branch line layout. In the fork alone we have the substantial signal box, a grounded coach body (four or six wheel), turntable (actually taken out some years before closure of the shed), the shed itself with its adjoining office, a huge water tank (somewhat similar to that Airfix kit produced some years ago) with a wooden hut virtually beneath, and a brick-built lineside hut which was no doubt for the use of the platelayers looking after this once important junction. You could run anything except 'Kings' through here!

Landore shed on 16th June 1957 with visiting 'Castle' No.4090 DORCHESTER CASTLE, from Old Oak Common, taking centre stage and showing off its recently acquired double chimney. This Swansea depot had two sheds, a four road dead-ended building opened by the GWR in 1874. That place is out of frame to the right. The shed in view was built in 1932 and had four through roads just leading out of the rear of the shed whilst a fifth road ended in a small repair shop. The coaling stage was sited behind the photographer's position. For a Sunday morning the depot is sparsely populated. Closed in June 1961, the whole depot site was flattened and a new diesel depot was erected for opening in 1963. *David Dalton.*

25

A close-up of some of the residents on that Sunday afternoon in June 1954. *KRP 5H.8.3.*

(*opposite*) Danygraig shed on Sunday afternoon, 13th June 1954 with its usual complement of small tank engines gathered from a number of sources including Swansea Harbour Trust, Llanelly & Mynydd Mawr, Powlesland & Mason, the entire batch of GWR Collett '1101' class, various sizes of 'Pannier' tank, with a 42XX class 2-8-0 keeping them all company. Situated just to the east of Swansea, the substantial stone built four-road running shed had a northlight pattern roof which actually faced northwards, and was opened in 1896 by the Rhonda & Swansea Bay Railway. The much taller building attached to the south side of the shed was a repair shop for locomotives and latterly wagons which had their own dedicated repair shop attached to the south side of that structure. When the depot closed to steam in January 1960, the five remaining '1101' class four-coupled tanks were withdrawn en masse, the sixth engine, No.1101 itself, having succumb some weeks previously. British Railways closed the place entirely in March 1964 when it was let out for industrial use. *KRP 5H.8.6.*

27

A low winter sun elongates the early afternoon shadows at Cardiff's Radyr shed in February 1958. The three residents on view, all relative newcomers, were 0-6-0PT No.3403, 56XX 0-6-2T No.6669 and 'Prairie' No.4177. Like many other sheds in this part of the Region, Radyr's whole allocation - more than fifty strong - consisted entirely of tank locomotives with the smallest represented by twenty-odd 'Panniers' and the largest by three 72XX class 2-8-2T. Shortly after Radyr became a main shed, it also became home for all ten of the recently delivered 34XX class 0-6-0PT but to spoil the party just after it had begun, No.3400 left for Shrewsbury and never returned. Up to December 1957 Radyr had been a sub shed of Cardiff Cathays shed, 88A, but by the new year Cathays had changed to sub-shed status whilst Radyr became 88A. In October 1960 the shed code was changed to 88B but Radyr kept that coding until closure in July 1965. Yet another of the Loan Act sheds, Radyr was opened in September 1931 having replaced a smaller Taff Vale shed dating from 1865. After closure the depot was used for stabling diesel locomotives, the shed building remaining intact. *David Dalton.*

The overflow sidings at Radyr shed during a summer visit in the early 1960s with the usual collection of medium and large tank engines on view. *David Dalton.*

29

On a rather quiet shed yard, 56XX class No.5608 is prepared for its next duty at Treherbert on Sunday 12th August 1956. Although only a section of the four-road engine shed is in view, it is easy to see the Loans Act type of design employing corrugated asbestos cladding over a lightweight steel framework, set on a brick bund wall. This building, so similar to many others put up by the GWR during the late Twenties and early Thirties, was erected in 1931 and replaced a stone built semi-roundhouse (half) shed which had been erected at Treherbert by the Taff Vale Railway in 1866. The original shed handed over a number of TVR locomotives to the GW-built shed in 1931 and many of those - 'O4' class - were still active when British Railways came into being and consisted more than half of the allocated forty-odd engines - all tank engines incidentally and mostly 0-6-2 type. No.5608 was one of regular GWR examples which gradually superseded the pre-Group engines which had all left by February 1956. Treherbert shed itself, still coded 88F, was closed on 1st March 1965 when just four locomotives were left on its books - they all went to Pontypool Road but not for long because that shed too closed during the following May. *David Dalton.*

This former Great Western outpost at Crewe Gresty Lane was tucked away at the bottom of the embankment of the Crewe to Shrewsbury main line. Opened in 1870, it was doubled in length during 1913 and closed fifty years later in June 1963. This is the un-coded depot on 5th March 1961 with 'Hall' No.4921 EATON HALL enjoying the facility of a quiet Sunday when nobody other than railway enthusiasts seemed to be about the place. Most 'spotters' visiting Crewe on a Sunday would make the trek to this little shed (South shed was not far anyway) to hopefully 'cop' between four and six 'namers' simmering away over the weekend. The presence of the WD 'Austerity' would no doubt have drawn a few groans from most but it was rare to find one of the 2-8-0s on Gresty Lane. *David Dalton.*

The three road stone built northlight engine shed at Llantrisant was opened by the GWR in October 1900 and replaced an earlier two road dead-ended shed erected by the Ely Valley Railway in 1860. All the facilities except the turntable are in view here on 28th July 1957, along with a couple of unidentified 0-6-0PT. The shed was coded 86D by the Western Region but in October 1960 it changed to 88G with closure taking place in October 1964. During BR days the allocation consisted exclusively tank engines and besides sixteen or more 'Panniers' the depot also housed a couple of the 14XX 0-4-2T until they were sent away individually in 1952 and 1958. For a short while, until May 1951, the Alexandra Docks & Railway 2-6-2T No.1205 was resident prior to its transfer to Canton. Of course being associated with the movement of coal trains, Llantrisant also had a handful of heavyweight motive power in the shape of 42XX class 2-8-0 tanks. *David Dalton.*

32

Although situated on the GWR/LNWR Joint line linking Shrewsbury and Hereford, Leominster engine shed only supplied motive power to the three branches radiating from the small Herefordshire town which appropriately was also known as Leominster Junction at various times. The shed in this 19th July 1959 view was the second such building housing motive power here; the first shed, also a two-road affair, was opened in 1853 by the S&HR but was demolished in 1901 to make way for station enlargements. This was the replacement shed, complete with a northlight (although in this case it is certainly a southlight) roof, situated on the east side of the main line just north of the station. Regular occupant 0-6-0PT No.7437 resides inside the shed whilst another of the class sits on the turntable road - note the luxury of a coaling crane. The nearest branch was that to Kington which also required an engine to be outstationed at Kington where a small one-road shed housed the engine working the trains to Presteign and New Radnor. The next branch was that to Tenbury Wells which left the main line some miles north of Leominster at Woofferton junction, whilst the final branch, that to Bromyard and Worcester, diverged south-eastwards from the main line just south of the station. For the services on these branches the usual motive power in BR days consisted 0-6-0PT working both freight and passenger trains, alongside motor fitted 14XX 0-4-2T which not only worked the passenger services but could often be seen with mixed trains at the western end of the Kington branch. However, even before Dr Beeching came along, BR recognised that all these branches were loss making and from September 1952 the Leominster to Bromyard passenger service was withdrawn. Less than three years later, in February 1955, the branch to Kington was closed to passenger traffic. Although the loss of the passenger engines affected Leominster shed slightly, it remained operational to service and house the engine working the Tenbury branch and the Ludlow auto, and that shunting the station and local yard, and that handling any goods traffic on the Kington line. All the engines were supplied by Hereford shed. In July 1961 the Tenbury Wells line was closed from Woofferton junction and another of Leominster's duties disappeared. The inevitable closure took place on 2nd April 1962; demolition followed. *David Dalton.*

An undated photograph of the square roundhouse at Tondu (86F) shows the weekend situation at that place where lack of stabling room meant that engines were left out in the cold. This is the eastern aspect of the shed showing the rebuilt northlight roof as supplied by the Western Region in 1953 complete with corrugated asbestos cladding and some large circular ventilators as preferred by the WR. The shed itself dates from 1889 and was built by the GWR to replace a much smaller shed put up by the Ogmore Valley Railway in 1865. The lines curving off to the left went to Tondu station whilst just off picture to the right another set of tracks led to Tondu North junction, connected by lines on the other, west side of the engine shed. Ogmore junction was behind the photographer. 'Pannier' No.9660 was allocated to 86F throughout the 1950s so there are no clues there as to the date but it was probably early 60s looking at the state of the weathered wall cladding. However, another photograph taken on the same day shows 42XX 2-8-0T No.4262 and 0-6-0PT No.4675 both with 88H shed plates! That was Tondu's new code from October 1960. Both of those engines worked until 1964 and 1965 respectively, No.9660 until November 1964. This shed closed in February 1964 and was later demolished. *David Dalton.*

The former London & North Western engine shed at Swansea Paxton Street became part of the Western Region soon after nationalisation. The depot's its geographical position, in the south-west of Wales and deep inside former GWR territory, making it politically sensible to hand the facility over to the WR. Known variously as Paxton Street or Victoria, the former title was the correct one because the original engine shed known as Victoria was sited nearer to Victoria passenger station and was closed in January 1882 when the new six-road, northlight shed at the end of Paxton Street opened. The shed entered 1948 with the same shed code it had been designated by the LMS but in 1949, once the WR had sorted out their own coding using the former LMS principal adopted by BR, the code became 87K. The depot started life under the WR regime with a mixture of pre and post Grouping LMS types including some former Midland 0-6-0T alongside the large ex LNWR 0-8-0 tender engines. To finish off the mix, more than a dozen WD Austerity 2-8-0s were also shedded there. As the decade ground on, the allocation changed somewhat as WR 'Panniers' were drafted in to replace the ex MR and LMS 0-6-0 tanks. The 'Austerities' were sent packing in favour of Stanier 2-8-0s (half of those were Swindon built examples too). This view sums up the allocation by the summer of 1954 when this Webb 'Coal Tank' No.58924, which had just transferred from Abergavenny, was hanging on to life by a thread only to be summoned to Crewe and oblivion in September. Another recent Abergavenny transfer was the Stanier Cl.3 No.40105, seen in the middle of the pack. Note 'Pannier' No.7439 which was one of the first WR engines acquired by 87K. The depot was closed at the end of August 1959 and any former LNWR influence in this part of Wales was extinguished. *KRP 4F.8.6.*

To serve the steel producing district around Port Talbot, the Port Talbot Railway provided an engine shed at Duffryn junction in 1896. The five road shed was actually large enough for a sixth road but it was left to the GWR to install the final set of rails during improvements carried out in 1931. From the outset it was known as Duffryn Yard and by BR days, as 87B, it housed a mixture of tank engines large and small, numbering between fifty and sixty, the majority being the ubiquitous 'Pannier'. This 13th June 1954 picture shows a couple of the shed's larger engines stabled at the east end of the yard with a somewhat picturesque background; whereas the aspect looking to the west would reveal heavy industry in the shape of gas holders, chimneys, rolling mills and everything associated with the manufacture of steel. 42XX class 2-8-0T No.4265 spent the whole of the decade working from 87B along with nine or ten others of the class. Later they were joined by a couple of the even larger 72XX 2-8-2T. Situated in between the 0-6-0PTs and the eight-coupled giants were a dozen or so 0-6-2T. Duffryn Yard closed in March 1964 and later demolished. *KRP 5H.8.7.*

2251 class 0-6-0 No.2256 spent the weekend of 26th and 27th June 1954 stabled on this radiating road south of the turntable at Banbury engine shed. With nearly seventy locomotives allocated it was impossible for the Oxfordshire depot to house even a half of the complement on the four shed roads. The shed building, the rear gable of which can be glimpsed in the background, was opened by the GWR in October 1908 and replaced a smaller shed, dating from 1889, on the north side of the main line. The importance of Banbury came to the fore during W.W.II when the Allied build-up to D-Day started some eighteen months before the event and trains of stores, munitions and a multitude of war materials were transported through the county towards the southern counties. Banbury engine shed hosted many visiting locomotives from other companies, besides the WD and USATC locomotives on loan to Britain's railways at that time. Although the intensity of the wartime traffic dropped away in the post-war years, Banbury kept a sizeable allocation of freight and mixed traffic locomotives throughout the first decade of BR ownership. Even when closure came in October 1966 there was a respectable number of the BR Standard 9F 2-10-0s sent from Banbury to other depots. In 1963 the depot had changed allegiance from the Western Region (84C) to London Midland Region (2D) and this boundary change probably gave the shed a further lease of life, for instance, its small stud 'Britannia' Pacifics, acquired after becoming 2D, were handling traffic such as the Nottingham (Victoria) to London (Marylebone) express and semi-fast passenger services as part of a complicated diagram which required locomotives with high capacity tenders. What of No.2256 here; apart from a couple of months spent at Westbury in the summer of 1955, it stayed at 84C throughout the decade. *KRP 6F.8.1.* 37

Birkenhead engine shed was a joint affair initially with the L&NWR and latterly the LMS. British Railways were not too sure about its status in either the LMR or WR. By 1951 the situation was sorted out and shed became LMR responsibility even though its still housed more than forty ex-GWR locomotives amongst the ninety-odd engines allocated. On 31st October 1954 the shed still had numerous former GW types allocated including this 14XX 0-4-2T No.1457, which it appears had been forgotten about by the WR authorities or perhaps they were leaving it be for as long as possible to remind the LM authorities whose locomotives they were sharing the shed with. Apparently the WR had this engine down as allocated to 84J Croes Newydd but perusal of the shed plate will see that 6C is plainly visible! 51XX No.5176 was definitely acknowledged by the WR as belonging to 6C but it left Birkenhead in March 1957 for the friendlier climes of Stourbridge. *KRP 26H.8.6.*

Birkenhead shed yard 6th March 1955. Six months on from the previous view and 6C is still housing locomotives with GWR on their side tanks - seven years after the end of Grouping. This is 2-6-2T No.4129 one of nine such 41XX 'Prairie' tanks still allocated to Birkenhead but they all left together in March 1957 along with the solitary 51XX. The four 'Grange' class 4-6-0, Nos.6831, 6841, 6859, and 6878, which were still allocated in 1955 all left in June 1958. Two 'Panniers' and an unidentified tank engine make up this little formation which were probably on a yard shunt. Note the newly built concrete ash plants rising in the background as part of the London Midland modernisation of Birkenhead depot. Further views of Birkenhead, including an overall view of the two engine sheds which comprised this depot will appear in the LMR volume in this series - after all, its only right to give both regions a bite of the cherry! *David Dalton.*

This is the Cardiff Cathays coaling stage on 21st August 1955 with 94XX 0-6-0T No.8469 having its bunker topped up with some choice coal by the two on-duty coalmen. The stage was one of the 1929 'improvements' carried out by the Great Western at this depot. During the same period the LNER and the LMS were installing mechanical coaling plants at their main and secondary engine sheds; Cathays would have been regarded as secondary by those two companies but its large allocation of seventy plus locomotives and intensity of their workload would have certainly given it the status for modernisation to mechanical plant. Alas, the shed never did receive any kind of modernisation to service steam locomotives and it plodded on July 1958 when the last of them transferred to other depots. Cathays did however receive modernisation of sorts when it was converted to house diesel multiple units at their introduction to Cardiff services in 1958. *KRP 93F.6.*

21st August 1955 - On your way over the footbridge which spanned the eastern yard of Canton engine shed, you notice an approaching westbound express which has just departed Cardiff (General) and although you can't wait to view the locomotive yard it would only take a few seconds to stop and wait and observe which engine is heading the passenger train. There you go, click - 5925 EASTCOTE HALL - in the bag. It was one of Canton's own which, given a few more minutes, would have been missed and it would not be coming back to Cardiff today. So it was a good idea to stop and observe its passing - another cop. Okay, what are those engines alongside the eastern coaling stage? Oh yes, the long building on the left! That was, up to about 1930, a carriage shed but it was converted into a milk depot and latterly handled parcels traffic too. *KRP 94F.5.*

Running in from a general overhaul at Barry works, Newton Abbot based 45XX No.5573 looks rather smart on Canton yard on Tuesday 21st March 1961. Evidence of renewal for the northlight roof appears to be fairly recent and earlier photographs suggest the straight shed was re-roofed circa 1955. The whole place was closed to steam in September 1962 and a new diesel depot was built on the site of the roundhouse. *David Dalton.*

Looking far from smart, Bristol Bath Road 'County' No.1028 COUNTY OF WARWICK gets some attention in Canton shed yard before working back home, circa 1953. There are a couple of other, unrelated, things worth noting in this picture. On the extreme left, the little hut, alongside the big hut, must rank (even by BR standards of the time) as one of the most ramshackle structures ever. There is every possibility that it may have been used by the contractors rebuilding the roof of the six-road straight shed during this period but nevertheless it has great modelling potential, assuming you could reproduce its 'wavy' appearance. Secondly, note the hoist which was part of the footbridge structure - can anybody enlighten us as to the history of that appliance? *David Dalton.*

43

Newport's Ebbw Junction engine shed consisted two square roundhouses and a large multi-bay repair shop which became operational in July 1915. Its allocation was made up in the main from freight locomotives both tender and tank types, along with a large number of 0-6-0PT and, for good measure, some 'namers' from the 'Grange', 'Hall', and 'Saint' classes. Quite a mix and, at the start of BR, numbering in excess of 140 locomotives. The 2-6-2T was represented by four or five 51XX class engines besides a couple of the 31XX class as seen here on 21st August 1955. Centre stage is '3150' class No.3170 which had arrived at 86A in November 1954 from Severn Tunnel Junction shed. This engine was one of the original Churchward Swindon built examples from June 1907 and was to end its days at Ebbw Junction three years hence. *KRP 95F.3.*

No.3103 had been at 86A since before BR days and was another of the Churchward '3150' examples but which had been rebuilt by Collett just prior to W.W.II to incorporate smaller wheels and higher boiler pressure for banking purposes. No.3103 lasted a bit longer than its unrebuilt sister and was not withdrawn until January 1960, again whilst still allocated to Ebbw Junction. Note that the left corner of the coaling stage has brickwork which was 'open' to allow for further extension of the building. In the event the extension was never proceeded with but instead an extension at the other (south) end of the stage was erected in the style of the Loan Act sheds incorporating an asbestos clad steel frame on a dwarf or bund brick wall. By 1955 the structure was suffering somewhat. *KRP 95F.2.*

Under the shadow of the transporter bridge spanning the River Usk, a pair of 2-8-0Ts, No.4201 and ex works No.5231 stable on the north side of the depot precincts at Newport Pill engine shed on Sunday, 21st August 1955. The lone, unidentified, 'Pannier', represented the other half of the allocation at this shed which at this period consisted approximately thirty-four 0-6-0PT, and about twenty 2-8-0T. Up to November 1954 the two Alexandra Docks 0-6-0Ts Nos.666 and 667 had appropriately resided here but No.667 was condemned that month and some five months later No.666 followed. The northlight pattern, two-road, shed had been opened in 1898 by the Alexandra (Newport & South Wales) Dock & Railway Co. and thrived for so many years until the march of modernisation saw the last of its steam locomotives transfer away in 1963 to make way for the diesel shunters which came and then quickly went. The inevitable demolition did not take place for some years afterwards. One of the nice things about visiting steam sheds on a Sunday was the fact that you were virtually guaranteed to find a full house because the nature of the steam locomotive meant that it had to come home for servicing, wash-outs, refuelling and minding - you could not switch them off and leave them, they required constant attention. Rough on the authorities, great for the enthusiast. *KRP 96F.1.*

The north end of Aberystwyth shed yard contained this large modern hoist which was able to lift one end of a locomotive sufficient to extract the driving wheels. On 23rd October 1955 it appears to be ready to lift a 'Prairie' tank which has been positioned in the right spot for such an operation. That such equipment was available at a depot which was essentially a sub shed was virtually unheard of on British Railways but, the geographical isolation of the western section of the Cambrian lines made such an investment necessary. Hogging the picture is one of our old friends 'Dukedog' No.9022 which still had nearly two years of operational life in front of it when this scene was captured on film. The GWR invested heavily at Aberystwyth. In 1938 this two road shed was opened to replace the old Cambrian establishment which dated from 1864 and had stood on the same site. A new coaling stage and 55ft turntable were provided at the same time. When BR standard gauge steam vacated the shed in April 1965 the building was utilised for the narrow gauge locomotives working the Vale of Rheidol line and is, apparently, still performing that function now. *KRP 107H.7.*

Turned, coaled, watered and prepared for its next working, Machynlleth based 'Manor' No.7803 HARCOTE MANOR graces the yard outside Aberystwyth shed on 23rd October 1955. Note the choice lumps of coal stacked carefully onto the tender. By now the 4-6-0 is wearing the dull unlined black livery of the period complete with the large version of the BR emblem. During much of the BR period Machynlleth shed was the parent shed to Aberystwyth, the latter sub shed had, however, the lion's share of the 'Manor' allocation which was used constantly by the nearby terminus station which relied on their services for hauling the Shrewsbury bound, and beyond, express passenger and mail trains besides those hauling trains southwards to Carmarthen; this latter routes' services were usually taken care of by the Carmarthen and later Llanelly based contingent of the class. *KRP 108H.7.*

The eastern aspect of Aberystwyth shed on 23rd October 1955 with the ubiquitous 'Pannier' - No.7417, a 'Dukedog' - No.9025, a 'Manor' - No.7802 and a 43XX - No.4377. No.7802 has what appears to be graffiti on its open smokebox door but the chalked message actually reads 'to be cleaned'. The 0-6-0PT has already been cleaned but the rear sheet of the coal bunker really shows the engine off nicely with fire irons, lamps and even a bucket hanging off the various hooks thereon. No.7417 was one of a pair of 'lightweight' 0-6-0PTs allocated to Machynlleth at this time and was sub-shedded at Aberystwyth for working both goods and passenger trains as required. The 4-4-0 was a regular visitor to the coast from Oswestry albeit not for much longer. Our 2-6-0 on the left was a newcomer to the area and had only just transferred to Machynlleth from Westbury, via a few weeks at Chester. No.4377 has yet to acquire a shedplate but it was to spend the rest of its life working from 89C. The stationary boiler with the rather tall chimney kept the sand supplies dry in what is basically a seaside town. As sub sheds go, Aberystwyth must have been one of the largest on the Western Region, if not British Railways although some of those in the South Wales valleys regularly stabled greater numbers of locomotives at weekends. However, a number of the Aberystwyth workings could have been described as 'important' and they include the CCE and the York Mails. Finally, how many sub sheds had their own locomotive hoist? *KRP 108H.8.*

The Vale of Rheidol locomotive facility at Aberystwyth on Sunday 23rd October 1955. On the left is the running shed with No.8 just visible in the gloom, whilst No.9 was further inside the shed. The building on the right was the repair shop which, it will be noted, was somewhat wider and gave fitters a bit more room in which to work. Where the two sheds joined the party wall cladding had been taken down to allow easy egress between running shed and repair shop! No.7 was lurking in the latter shed according to Keith Pirt's notes. These two buildings were erected in 1902 for the lines' two locomotives and served the railway - which had changed hands to Cambrian control in 1913, GWR in 1922, and finally to BR in 1948 - until 1965 when the standard gauge locomotive shed near Aberystwyth main line station was adapted to house the three narrow gauge locomotives. With the move across town for the narrow gauge V-o-R, the buildings were surplus were dismantled; they didn't look too sturdy even in 1955! The water tank was a Great Western addition and has all the hallmarks of their standard tanks except its profile was lower than normal. Of course, in 1955 neither of the three locomotives carried a name and were simply 7, 8, and 9. *KRP 109H.2.*

In July 1963 things, other than the locomotive shed, had changed on the V-o-R railway. All three of the 'Prairies' had acquired names, lined green livery adorned the 25-ton bulk of each one and the line was enjoying a rise in popularity from tourism, and the attention of railway enthusiasts. Named in June 1956, the three Swindon built tank engines became:- No.7 OWAIN GLYNDWR (of July 1923), No.8 LLYWELYN (of July 1923), and No.9 PRINCE OF WALES (rebuilt from No.1213 in 1924), the latter name once carried by one of the original engines, No.2. The original engines, Nos.1 and 2, lost their names in 1915 but were renumbered just before Grouping when No.1 became No.1212, and No.2 became No.1213 under the Great Western in 1922. No.1213 was rebuilt at Swindon in 1924 when, amongst other modifications, the Stephenson valve gear was changed to Walschaerts valve gear but its number remained the same and was not changed to No.9 until 1949 when British Railways did the honours. No.1, as No.1212, was scrapped in 1932 leaving just three locomotives to work the traffic. Ready for a days work; this is a well turned-out No.9 wearing the BR Brunswick green and probably in its best livery because some year later all three engines were repainted to BR blue! Note that the water tank has also acquired a fresh coat of paint but no such luck for the shed building. *KRP 295.2.*

Aberystwyth - Two Oswestry (89D) based tender engines, a nicely turned-out 'Manor' and scruffy 32XX class leader No.3200 soak up the morning sunshine at Aberystwyth in July 1963. Behind No.7810 is another Manor, albeit unknown. By this time in their lives, and from hereon to withdrawal, the 'Manors' were finding employment at a number of sheds which had hitherto seen nothing or very little of their ilk, Cardiff East Dock, Didcot, Landore, Llanelly, Neyland, Stourbridge, Swindon, Whitland, and for possibly the shortest allocation - Severn Tunnel Junction where No.7804 spent just a few weeks in August/September 1965 prior to being condemned. Not only were they employed by the WR, the Southern often seconded them for their own ends whenever a 'Manor' worked into the SR territory. However, back to our image here. When the CAMBRIAN COAST EXPRESS was retimed in 1960, it enabled the engine or engines working the Up morning train from Aberystwyth to Shrewsbury to then work the Down train back to Aberystwyth in the day, with just under an hour to service the train engine or engines at Shrewsbury shed. Some last minute oiling is being undertaken by the driver of DRAYCOTT MANOR prior to the 4-6-0 moving off to the terminus (which can be seen in the right background) where a full and arduous day awaited No.7810. *KRP 295.3.*

Machynlleth, 23rd October 1955. This covered coaling stage in one of the damper locations of west Wales must have been something of a luxury to the coalmen at Machynlleth. The girder framed construction was covered in corrugated iron and even had guttering and downspouts as an added bonus. Note that 0-4-2T No.5801 is still wearing its former identity some eight years after Nationalisation - something of a record? Looking rather smart, the tank was a recent acquisition from Brecon shed and was to end its days at 89C being withdrawn at the end of the summer timetable in 1958; I wonder if it still wore GWR. Keeping it company at Machynlleth were two other members of the class which were also newcomers to the area - Nos.5803 and 5809. Two of the similar, but motor-fitted, 14XX class 0-4-2T were also in residence at 89C during the early Fifties' but they had moved on to sheds in England by 1956. The two coal wagons in the frame are also looking fairly decent considering their occupation, the vehicle just inside the coaling shed particularly looks to be ex-works after repair. *KRP 108H.3.*

Machynlleth, 23rd October 1955. If you wanted to see a 'Dukedog' during BR days you headed for Machynlleth where you were guaranteed a sighting of any number of the seventeen members of the class which could be found working from this former Cambrian Railway outpost during the early and mid Fifties. This is No.9012 poking out of the western end of the shed shortly before withdrawal in July 1957. The NOT TO BE MOVED sign may well be an indication of the 4-4-0s impending doom. Note also the capuchon on its chimney is showing signs of deterioration. *KRP 108H.5.*

Two more different examples of the motive power residing at Machynlleth during BR days. On 4th April 1958, stabled at the south end of the shed yard, 45XX class 2-6-2T No.4549 was one of fifteen of its type allocated during the early years whilst the unidentified BR Standard Cl.2 was one of half a dozen such engines drafted in to replace the ageing 'Dukedog' 4-4-0s. *David Dalton.*

The four (see Oswestry, page 58) 'Manors' at Machynlleth shed in late July 1963. Could this same scene be re-enacted today? There is no reason why that should not be the case is there? *KRP 297.3.*

Full house at Machynlleth in July 1963 with 'Manors' hogging the yard and BR Standard 2-6-2T No.82005 billowing smoke outside the three-road section at the southern end of the shed. *KRP 298.1.*

On show are three rather immaculate 'Manors' stabled inside a very clean Oswestry engine shed in July 1963. Nos.7822 and 7828 are identified by their numbers but the third member of the trio is not; there was also a fourth 'Manor' hiding behind. These engines had been prepared for a special working, and double-headed at that. They are paired as 7828 and 7827 alongside 7822 and 7819 which is unseen behind. The event, where all four engines were employed was a Royal train working to and from the Cambrian coast, a duty which passed off without a hitch. All four of these engines passed into preservation and to have all four together in one picture (okay so we can't see 7819 but see also Machynlleth, page 56) must be something approaching unique especially as, at the time, they were all some years away from withdrawal. Oswestry engine shed started life in 1860 when the Oswestry & Newtown Railway opened this four-road shed. The Cambrian Railway absorbed the O&NR some four years later and then at some time before 1900 they added another, smaller two-road shed (visible through the archway) to the east side of the original building. The whole lot was re-roofed by the Western Region shortly after BR came into being, hence the tidy appearance of the interior of the building. *KRP 297.1.*

Some of the more usual occupants of Oswestry engine shed in BR days. Former Cambrian Railway '15' class 0-6-0 No.895, stables outside two-road extension circa 1952. All but three of the eleven survivors of the Cambrian 0-6-0s which became BR property were allocated to Oswestry; the others worked from the other end of the system at Machynlleth. Withdrawn in September 1954 along with the Nos.849 and 852, No.895's demise rendered the class extinct. Note the similarity between the '15' class and the Great Central J10 class, even the tender has an unmistakable likeness. *David Dalton.*

At an unknown date during late BR days in the south-west of Wales we see the south end of Neyland engine shed with three of its allocation stabled outside. All three of the 'Panniers' are unidentified but they are coaled-up ready for work so we can only assume this photograph was taken on a Sunday, or Saturday afternoon towards the end of the shed's life. Opened in 1856 by the South Wales Railway, the timber shed had an extension added before 1862 when the Great Western absorbed the SWR. Remarkably, the building survived to closure of the depot in September 1963 although being of timber construction it would have been easy enough to renew individual sections as they deteriorated over the century or more of its existence; the front wall had corrugated cladding (both asbestos and steel) during the last decade of the shed's existence. From a northern aspect the engine shed looked more like a range of farm buildings with three different heights and profiles on offer. In this undated view a wagon is poking out of the building, perhaps signifying that the shed was no longer in use for locomotive purposes. A 65ft turntable, out of frame to the left of the shed, was provided during 'modernisation' by the GWR in 1932 but otherwise the place remained pretty much as it had done in 1900. With the terminal station behind the photographer, the main line to the north and the rest of the BR network lay beyond the iron-railed fence behind the 0-6-0Ts. However, the closure of the engine shed was a foretaste of events to overtake Neyland's railway infrastructure and during the following December the goods facilities were closed down whilst six months later the passenger station sent out its last train. Throughout the 1950's Neyland had an allocation of forty or more locomotives, quite substantial for a depot with a small wooden running shed, especially considering that eight or so 4-6-0s were amongst that throng; 'County' class Nos.1001, 1020, 1027 and 1029 became virtual permanent fixtures throughout that decade. The fact that a railway ever existed here is impossible to find except for two road names - Station Road, which basically borders the land on which the railway yards stood (given over to a boat yard), and Railway Terrace which is situated just to the west of the area whereupon the engine shed once stood. *David Dalton.*

A sub shed to Swindon, Chippenham was one of the oldest engine sheds still standing when the Western Region came into being. The stone walls are original and perhaps the roof was too, in this circa 1954 picture, but the timber facade was a later addition and was in dire need of repair or renewal. The shed dated from 1858 and apparently was once home to broad gauge locomotives prior to its conversion to house standard gauge. The place looks like something you might come across in Mexico or some Third World country where steam locomotion has only just finished - derelict before closure. A Swindon allocated 0-6-0PT, No.4612, peers out of the gloom while three other tank engines hide further inside the shed. One regular working for Swindon allocated 14XX 0-4-2Ts based at Chippenham was the auto-train service over the five-mile branch to Calne (opened 2nd November 1863, closed 20th September 1965). Sited just north of the station on the Up side of the main line, Chippenham engine shed does not appear to have had any investment, during the 20th century anyway, by either the GWR or BR. It is believed to have closed its doors in early March 1964 in this same or perhaps worse condition. *David Dalton.* 61

This is 'Castle' No.7021 at Worcester engine shed in April 1963. The 4-6-0 has just pulled up at the coaling chute, a mechanical device which lifted the coal in a skip from below ground level to the lip of the chute where it was then tipped to allow the contents to fall into the tender by gravity. This was about as mechanical as the Great Western and later, the Western Region, ever got when it came to coaling locomotives. *Don Beecroft.*

The rear yard of the four-road shed - known as the goods engine shed - at Worcester appears to offer a peaceful ambience in this June 1964 setting with 'Prairie' No.6140 in near solitary confinement. In the event it never did work again and was withdrawn shortly after this photograph was captured. Evidence of the British Railways re-roofing of this particular shed can be seen in the new brick gable. Already the weeds are showing in the yard but it would be another eighteen months before they could grow in profusion, undisturbed. *Don Beecroft.* 63

The three-road shed - apparently known as the passenger engine shed - at Worcester in June 1964 with 'Grange' No.6937 FORTHAMPTON GRANGE alongside 'Pannier' No.3682. Both of the sheds here remained operational until steam was eliminated from the establishment in December 1965 after which the three-road building was utilised for diesel locomotives whilst the old 'goods engine shed' fell into disuse. *Don Beecroft.*

Many closed engine sheds became convenient temporary dumping grounds for withdrawn or stored locomotives. Such was the case at Upper Bank, Swansea where the former Midland Railway depot played host to these two unidentified 'Panniers' in 1963. The shed had closed in February of that year after a lifetime of housing 0-6-0 tank engines of both Midland and LMS origin although ex GWR 0-6-0PTs started to penetrate its boundary shortly after it became part of the Western Region officially, as sub to 87K - nearby Swansea Paxton Street shed. Later, after Paxton St. closed it became sub to 87D - Swansea East Dock. Since the LMS had re-organised its motive power department in 1935 Upper Bank had maintained a shed code of its own, 4C, with two sub sheds, Brecon and Gurnos but prior to that it was shed No.6 in the old Midland Railway and early LMS system. The Midland system did not work on numerical status but on geographical lines radiating straight out (sort of) from Derby, like sun beams, whereas Burton became No.2, Saltley No.3, Worcester No.4, Brecon No.5, and so on. For the record Toton was No.17 and Holbeck No.28 but you knew that already. This place was as far west that the Midland Railway got in Wales in their quest for a share of the lucrative coal trade. Upper Bank was opened in 1893 to replace a shed which came with the lease of the Swansea Vale Railway in 1874, a line which they absorbed in 1876. Initially a small wagon ramp sufficed as a coaling point at Upper Bank, the MR never did invest too much into their outposts of the vast empire but the LMS saw fit to cover the area with a wooden shelter to give a semblance of comfort in this somewhat exposed location. So, what was behind those doors of the closed engine at Upper Bank in 1963? Somebody, somewhere knows, those cycles belonged to someone local who entered through the wicket gate to view the content. *David Dalton.*

Barry shed yard 21st August 1955 with former Taff Vale 'A' class 0-6-2Ts Nos.357 and 390 displaying a myriad of rivets in the midday sunshine. Both engines were allocated to 88C, as Barry was coded under the BR scheme, but whereas No.357 ended its day at Barry, being withdrawn in January 1956, No.390 moved on to Abercynon and survived a further eighteen months in passenger service. It ended up being amongst the last of the TVR 'A' class in service. *David Dalton.*

Just in case. The architect in charge of the building of Oxley's coaling stage must have been given those three words at the end of the instruction to include reservation for extension into his drawings for the coal stage. In the event, the extension was not required but nevertheless it would have been easy enough for bricklayers in any age to follow the courses set down when the stage was built in 1907 (see also Ebbw Junction and Old Oak Common). Visiting Oxley shed from Bristol circa 1955, 2-8-0 No.4703 has its tender topped up with sufficient fuel for the journey home, whenever that was, and appears to be following an exLMS Stanier locomotive away to the shed but more than likely both engines are stabled on the coaling road for want of shed space. *David Dalton.*

Pontypool Road shed - Tuesday, 26th March 1963. 0-6-2T No.6677 is showing all the signs of a withdrawn locomotive 'in store' since condemnation during the previous January. It appears that the 56XX was being used for spares and was slowly cannibalised to keep other more roadworthy members of its class in traffic. A fairly recent arrival at 86G from Stourbridge, where it had worked throughout the BR period prior to its move to South Wales, No.6677 still wears the GWR initials some fifteen years after that company ceased to exist (on paper anyway)! Could it simply be layers of paint wearing away, including the two versions of BR emblems or did the engine manage to defy the painters for so long? Classmate No.6662 is probably stabled at the shed after working in on a train from Swansea. It is coaled and ready to return home, perhaps even hauling No.6677 off to a scrap yard somewhere but it was itself withdrawn in April and this may well have been its last outing. Perhaps it had even joined No.6677 'in store'. Pontypool Road engine shed closed in May 1965. *David Dalton.*

Shortly after it was withdrawn, 'Castle' No.4079 PENDENNIS CASTLE resides on the storage line at Westbury engine shed on Sunday 26th July 1964, along with a 'Pannier' and a 38XX 2-8-0, both unidentified but obviously withdrawn. The 4-6-0, latterly allocated to Swindon, was of course destined for preservation. *David Dalton.*

Yet another engine shed in a valley bottom was to be found at Ferndale, which was also the location of the penultimate passenger station (opened June 1876, closed June 1964) on the branch to Maerdy. This shed was opened by the Taff Vale Railway in 1884 as a four road dead-end affair built from local stone. It had two high pitched roofs topped with smoke ventilators, and planked gables. A timber clad coaling stage, built to the same design as the engine sheds completed the facilities. An earlier shed, also built by the TVR, had been erected in 1866 but as the mines began their century long extraction of anthracite and coal the expanding traffic required more locomotives and its single road soon became inadequate. Changing traffic patterns, along with the opening and closing of coal mines during the depressed 1930s, saw the 1884 shed reduced in both importance and later, in stature when the GWR demolished half of the shed leaving just two roads covered. The remaining section was re-roofed with tall ventilators and a corrugated asbestos clad gable - much like the Loan Act sheds. In this view, taken circa September 1962, Treherbert based 0-6-2T No.5676 rests on the Ferndale shed yard. Others of its ilk would join it and some compulsory 'Panniers' during the weekend break. Note the FB target which informed interested parties just where this engine was working; other targets worn by engines working from Ferndale consisted a simple F with a number beneath. Like many engine sheds located in the valleys it was closed in September 1964 as the diesel fleet outgrew the steam allocation and the requirement for servicing points receded. Ferndale became just another empty site where steam had stood for nearly a century. *David Dalton.*

Super power at Cathays. 2-8-2T No.7205 lingers on the shed yard at Cardiff Cathays in 1958. A long time resident of 88A the big tank moved on to Radyr's allocation when Cathays became a sub shed in January 1958. Most of this fifty-four strong class of 8F tank engines were stationed in South Wales and all remained operational until the early 1960s when steam was eliminated from much of the Western Region. *David Dalton.*

On its way to earn a living whilst it can, 28XX class 2-8-0 No.2895 drifts over the Horton Road level crossing and past Horton Road engine shed at Gloucester in April 1963. To the engine's left is the south wall of the engine shed which dated from 1872. Beyond the tender is the coaling stage which was erected by the GWR in 1921 during yard improvements. In May 1964 the nearby former Midland shed at Barnwood was closed and the handful of former LMR engines still active joined the dwindling WR allocation at Horton Road. The shed was closed to steam on New Year's Day 1966, effectively eliminating steam from this part of the Western Region. However, steam locomotives were not finished with the shed just then as over the next couple of years literally hundreds of ex Southern Region and a good number of Western Region locomotives bound for South Wales scrap yards were staged through Gloucester whilst en route, the sidings at Horton Road seeing many new types albeit dead ones. After some modification and lots of demolition the shed, or rather its site, became a diesel stabling point for many years afterwards. *Don Beecroft.*